THE
BIG BAD
JOKE BOOK

PRESENTED BY

Zig and Zag

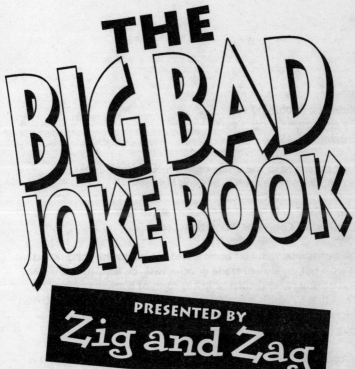

THE BIG BAD JOKE BOOK

PRESENTED BY Zig and Zag

Robinson Children's Books

Robinson Publishing Ltd
7 Kensington Church Court
London W8 4SP

First published in the UK by Robinson Children's Books,
an imprint of Robinson Publishing Ltd 1996

A copy of the British Library Cataloguing in Publications data is
available from the British Library.

ISBN 1 85487 478 0

Printed and bound in the EC

1 3 5 7 9 10 8 6 4 2

CONTENTS

This 'Big Bad Joke Book' is probably the most important invention since the 'Belly-button fluff extractor'. It doesn't tickle as much but it should certainly make you laugh as much! It took fourteen months of last year for us to fill this joke book with some of the most brilliantly zany and downright mad-in-the-head silly jokes that this Universe has to offer. We travelled from the Planet XJ9 to Chiswick compiling the jokes for you to enjoy.

So read on and giggle your socks off with our top of the range Bid Bad Joke Book.

Zig and Zag

7

Zig and Zag Go to School

PRIMARY SCHOOL PRANKS!

HARRY: I'm not going to school any more.
LARRY: Why's that?
HARRY: It's our teacher. On Monday she said 6 + 6 made 12. On Tuesday she said 8 + 4 made 12, and today she said 9 + 3 make 12. I'm not going back until she makes up her mind.

MUM: How did you enjoy your first day at school?
WILLY: First day? You mean I have to go back there again?

ZIG: How did you get on at school?
ZAG: Not too badly, except for this man called Sir who kept wanting us to do as he said.

The infants teacher was getting to know her new pupils. 'How old are you, Laura?' she asked one small girl.
'I'm not old, I'm almost new,' replied Laura indignantly.

11

TEACHER: Zig! Why are you always late?

ZIG: Because I threw away my alarm clock.

TEACHER: And why did you do that?

ZIG: Because it always went off when I was asleep.

Zig and Zag once visited a church school and had to say grace before lunch. 'Didn't you say a prayer before meals at home?' asked the headmaster. 'Certainly not,' replied Zag. 'Our Mum could cook.'

What does a teacher have that her class doesn't have?
The answers.

Did you hear about the class who decided to try to sell their teachers because they'd heard Old Masters fetched such a good price?

13

TEACHER: Give me a sentence starting with 'I'.
ZAG: I is . . .
TEACHER: No, Zag, we don't say 'I is', we say 'I am'.
ZAG: OK, I am the letter of the alphabet before J.

CHEMISTRY TEACHER: Who can explain what zinc is?
MOLLY: In our house it's where we wash ze dishes.

What's black and white and absolutely awful? A maths test paper.

Why is it dangerous to add up in the jungle?
Because if you add four and four you get ate.

15

Ben was rubbing his hands on the seat of his trousers. 'What's the matter?' asked Ken.

'I didn't write my essay last weekend.'

'So why are you rubbing the seat of your trousers?'

'Because when it comes to dealing with boys who don't write their essays when they should, our teacher believes in getting to the bottom of things.'

TEACHER: Stop showing off, Simon. Do you think you're the teacher here?

SIMON: No, sir.

TEACHER: Then stop behaving like a fool.

Why did the teacher switch on the lights?
Because her class was so dim.

16

What animals do you have to beware of
when you do exams?
Cheetahs.

One teacher always got angry with young Billy, who would sit sprawled at his desk with his feet out in the aisle, chewing gum. 'Billy!' he'd roar, 'take that gum out of your mouth and put your feet in this instant!'

TEACHER: Mary! Were you copying Sally's work?
MARY: No, I was just checking that she'd got mine right.

ENGLISH TEACHER: Did you write this verse, Kevin?
KEVIN: Yes, Miss.
ENGLISH TEACHER: Pleased to meet you, William Shakespeare.

TEACHER: Martin! You look very pale this morning. Are you feeling well?
MARTIN: Yes, Miss, I just gave my face a good wash.

ZIG: Our maths teacher likes me better than you.

ZAG: How do you know?

ZIG: She's put more kisses in my book.

ZIG: Do your teachers do bird impressions likes ours do?
ZAG: What do you mean?
ZIG: They watch us like hawks!

TEACHER: Charlie, your homework looks as if it was written by your brother John. Did he do it for you?
CHARLIE: No, sir. But I did borrow his pen.

Does an apple a day keep a teacher away? It does if your aim is good enough!

What do YOU call a deaf teacher?

Did you hear about the pupil who was told to do 100 lines and drew 100 cats on the paper?
He thought his teacher had said '100 lions'.

When is a naughty schoolboy like a postage stamp?
When he is licked and put in a corner.

MUSIC TEACHER: Are any of you quick at picking up music?

ZAG: Zig and I are, sir.

MUSIC TEACHER: Good, you two can help me move the piano.

GEOGRAPHY TEACHER: Who can tell me where Felixstowe is?

WINSTON: At the end of Felix's foot, Miss.

Anything you like, because he can't hear you.

23

TEACHER: Lots of things have come into being in the last 100 years. Who can name one really important thing that didn't exist 100 years ago?
TESSA: Me!

The teacher carefully explained to her class that 'can't' was short for 'cannot', and that the apostrophe meant that some letters were missing. 'Who can tell me what don't is short for?' she asked.
Clever Clogs Clara put up her hand.
'Doughnut, Miss?'

TERRY: You know what they say about the dinners at our school, don't you?
PERRY: No, what?
TERRY: What goes down must come up!

The English teacher told his class to write the longest sentence they could. One bright spark wrote 'life imprisonment'.

25

Did you hear about the cross-eyed teacher? She couldn't control her pupils.

26

What did Zag say when the teacher told him off
for putting a finger in his soup?
'It's all right, it isn't hot!'

TEACHER: Why are you always late for school,
Zig?
ZIG: Because you always ring the bell before I
get here.

TIM: I was top of the class today!
DAD: How did you manage that?
TIM: Because I answered a question about
hippos.
DAD: What was the question?
TIM: The teacher asked us how many legs
a hippo had, and I said six.
DAD: But that's not right.
TIM: I know, but it was the nearest
anybody got!

27

ENGLISH TEACHER: Who wrote 'To a Mouse'?
JENNY: I don't know, but I bet they didn't get an answer!

The class went to a concert, and afterwards Kelly asked the teacher why the members of the orchestra kept looking at their books while they played.
'Those books are the score,' replied the teacher.
'Really?' asked Kelly. 'Who won?'

ENGLISH TEACHER: Who can explain what a synonym is?
BARRY: It's a word you use in place of the one you can't spell.

What exams do horses take?
Hay-levels.

Why did the teacher wear dark glasses? Because her class was so bright!

KEN: How were your exam questions?
LEN: They were OK, it was the answers I had trouble with.

TEACHER: Why are you crossing the road at this dangerous junction? Can't you see there's a zebra crossing just down there?
MERVYN: I hope it's having better luck than I am!

Why did the pencils go to the doctor?
They had leadaches.

When Zig and Zag went round collecting for a swimming pool for their school, several people offered them buckets of water.

Why did the singing teacher stand on a chair?
So she could reach the high notes.

What's large, grey, wears a beard and writes on a blackboard?
An elephant disguised as a teacher.

ZIG: Did you really learn to speak Russian in six easy lessons?

ZAG: Yes, but the 200 that followed were quite difficult.

Who can tell the story of *Puss in Boots*?
It's about a cat in a chemist's shop.

33

TEACHER: Tell me ten animals that come from Africa.
BILLY: 'Er – nine lions and a hippo.

 **What was the first thing Queen Victoria did on coming to the throne? Sit down.**

What do you get if you cross a school burglar with a concrete mixer?
A hardened criminal.

TEACHER: Who can tell me what the Order of the Bath is?
JIMMY: In our house it's Mum, Dad, my sister, then me.

Why did the headmistress marry the school caretaker?
Because he swept her off her feet.

ZIG: Shall I tell you the joke about the pencil?

Why is a classroom like an old car?
Because it's full of nuts, and has a crank at the front.

TEACHER: What's the difference between an African elephant and an Indian elephant?
BEN: About 5,000 kilometres.

Why did Cuthbert have three pairs of glasses?
One for reading, one for distance, and one to look for the other two.

ZIG: Who invented the radio?
ZAG: Macaroni?

ZAG: Is there any point to it?

ZAG: What language do they speak in Cuba?
ZIG: Cubic?

What's brown, hairy, wears dark glasses and carries a pile of exercise books? A coconut disguised as a teacher.

What was the cold war?
A snowball fight.

TEACHER: Show me America on the map.

ZIG: There, Miss.

TEACHER: That's right. Now, Zag, who discovered America?

ZAG: Zig did.

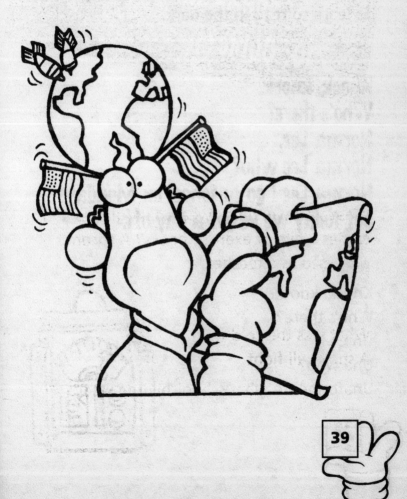

What's the best thing about going to school?
Coming home again!

Why do people go to night school?
To learn to read in the dark.

Knock, knock.
Who's there?
Norma Lee.
Norma Lee who?
Norma Lee I go to school on Mondays
but today we've got a day off.

Knock, knock.
Who's there?
Una.
Una who?
Unaforms are what schoolchildren wear.

**What do you call a
school jacket that's
on fire?
A blazer.**

What's the coldest
country in the world?
Chile.

Where do people
never get enough to
eat?
Hungary.

**Why are fish well
educated?
They live in schools.**

What's a carafe?

An African animal with a long neck.

COOKERY TEACHER: What are the best things to put in a Christmas cake?
ZIG AND ZAG: Your teeth!

TEACHER: What does 'illegal' mean?
DAVE: A sick bird of prey.

What's margarine?
Butter made from
imitation cows.

TEACHER: Today I'm
going to give you a
lesson on the
Himalayas.
JENNY: Will we be back
in time for *Neighbours*,
Miss?

43

TEACHER: Order, children, order!
CLASS: Hamburgers and fries all round, please.

TEACHER: If I had 20 twopence coins in my right trouser pocket and 20 penny coins in my left trouser pocket what would I have?
DAVEY: Heavy trousers, sir.

Why did the teacher call her dog Ginger?
Because Ginger snaps.

Have you heard about the school swot?
He killed more flies than anybody else!

44

What time is it when an elephant sits on your desk? Time to get a new desk!

TEACHER: I thought I told you to stand at the end of the line, Daniel!
DANIEL: You did, Miss, but there was someone there already.

What's the difference between an ice-cream and a school bully?
You lick one, the other licks you.

What did Zig shout when the teacher dropped the school bell?
'He just dropped a clanger!

45

MICK: Zig was teacher's pet last year.
NICK: Why was that?
MICK: She couldn't afford a dog.

'Why do you want to work in a bank when you leave school?'
'I've heard there's money in it.'

Why was Zig so bad at history?
He believed in letting bygones be bygones.

Why did Henry VIII have so many wives?
He liked to chop and change.

TEACHER: What's the French national anthem called?
MARY: The Mayonnaise.

What's yellow, lumpy and stupid?
Thick school custard.

TEACHER: Zig! Why are you always late?

ZIG: Because I threw away my alarm clock.

TEACHER: And why did you do that?

ZIG: Because it always went off when I was asleep.

Why is school like a shower?
One wrong turn and you're in hot water.

What's black and white and absolutely awful?
Zag's underwear. Sorry! Exams.

ZIG: It's time for your violin lesson.
ZAG: Oh, fiddle!

Why is an optician like a teacher?
Both test the pupils.

Why is school like a shower?
One wrong turn and you're in hot water.

Why did the teacher stand on her head? She was turning things over in her mind.

TEACHER: What does 'unaware' mean?
ZAG: It's what you put on first thing in the morning.

What do you call a Scotsman who serves school dinners?
Dinner Ken.

ZIG: I've thought of a way of making the football team play better.
ZAG: Does that mean you're leaving it?

SHARON: Have you been at this school all your life?
DARREN: Not yet!

What was King Arthur's
favourite game?
Knights and crosses.

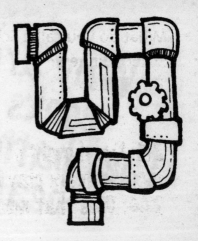

ZAG: What steps do you
take when a teacher's
on the rampage?
ZIG: Very long ones!

Did you hear about the class
from a city school who went
on a country ramble and
found a crate of milk bottles
in a village? They thought
they'd discovered a cow's nest!

51

Why are school cooks cruel? They batter fish and beat eggs.

BEN: The school trip went to Bury St Edmunds.
HEN: Is he dead?

What do you think about needlework?
Oh, only so-so.

What happened to the plant in the maths class?
It grew square roots.

52

TEACHER: What kind of food do pelicans eat?
ALEC: Anything that fits the bill.

When does a teacher become two teachers? When he's beside himself.

Why did the teacher stand on her head? She was turning things over in her mind.

Knock, knock.
Who's there?
Genoa.
Genoa who?
Genoa good school?

53

Zig and Zag Go Shopping

SHOPPING
MALL
MADNESS!

Why is a fish shop always crowded?
Because the fish fillet.

'May I try on that red shirt in the
window?' asked Zag.
'No, sir, you'll have to use the changing
room like everybody else.'

Where do loonies like Zig and Zag buy
their food?
Insanesbury's.

CUSTOMER IN RECORD SHOP:
Have you got 'Greensleeves'?
ASSISTANT: No, it's just the
lighting in here.

WOMAN IN BUTCHER'S SHOP: Have you got pigs' feet?
BUTCHER: No, my shoes are too tight.

Did you here about the florist who had two children?
One was a budding genius, the other a blooming idiot.

Why is your hand like a hardware shop? They both have nails.

Why did the chemist tiptoe past the medicine cupboard?
He didn't want to wake the sleeping pills.

58

What's the difference between a limp lettuce
and a miserable song?
One's a bad salad, the other's a sad ballad.

ZIG: Why have you got a lump on your head?
ZAG: A tomato hit me.
ZIG: But tomatoes are soft.
ZAG: This one was in a tin.

What salad
ingredient
plays snooker?
A cue-cumber.

How is cat food sold?
Purr can.

What did the dumbo do with the Manx cat?
Took it to a retail shop.

ZIG: Polar bears live on ice apparently.
ZAG: Not on fish then.

What sort of sweets
don't hurt your teeth?
Gums.

BARBER: Were you
wearing a red tie?
CUSTOMER: No.
BARBER: Oh dear.

What's another name
for a butcher's boy?
A chop assistant.

CUSTOMER: That cake looks as if it's
been nibbled by mice.
BAKER: That's impossible, the cat's been
lying on it all day.

61

Did you hear about the woman who rushed into the greengrocer's and asked for half a pound of mixed nuts, with not too many coconuts?

ZIG: It's a mile down the road to the supermarket.
ZAG: So what? To get there you just have to move two feet.

62

On what day does the baker sell pancakes?
Fry-day.

ZIG: Did you hear about the fight in the chip shop?
ZAG: No, what happened?
ZIG: A lot of fish got battered.

ZIG: I'd like to buy one of those instruments that sounds as if it belongs with cheese.
ZAG: What, a pickle-o?

When Zig and Zag went to buy a piano the man in the shop couldn't open it. The keys were inside, you see.

63

Zag tried to buy a pair of jeans.
'Certainly, sir, walk this way,' said the assistant.
ZIG: I'm not sure he wants them quite that tight.

What did the elephant buy at Burtons?
A grey suit.

What can you buy that has four legs but only one foot?
A bed.

ZIG: I'd like to buy a bed, please.
ASSISTANT: Certainly, sir. Spring mattress?
ZIG: Oh no, I want to use it all year round.

Why did the bed spread?
Because it saw the pillow slip.

SIGN ON A HAIRDRESSER'S SHOP:

WE WILL HELP YOU DYE.

SIGN IN A DELICATESSEN:

OUR TONGUE SANDWICHES SPEAK FOR THEMSELVES.

SIGN ON A TRAVEL AGENT'S:
PLEASE GO AWAY.

66

SIGN ON A HEALTH FOOD SHOP:
CLOSED DUE TO ILLNESS.

SIGN AT A CHIROPODIST'S:
WILLIAM THE CORN-CURER.

SIGN ON A MUSIC SHOP:
GUITARS FOR SALE, CHEAP, NO STRINGS ATTACHED.

67

SIGN ON A DEPARTMENT STORE: Bargain basement upstairs.

SIGN ON A MUSICIAN'S DOOR: Out Chopin, Back in a minuet.

68

SIGN ON A CHEMIST'S SHOP: We dispense with accuracy.

SIGN ON A BARBER'S: Haircutting while you wait. Hair cut for £2, children for £1.

Where does Frankenstein's wife have her hair done?
At the ugly parlour.

ZIG: I can only afford to go window shopping.
ZAG: How many did you buy?

What's a shoplifter? Someone who has the gift of the grab.

ZIG: Have you got holes in your socks?
ZAG: No.
ZIG: Then how do you get them on?

What do you call the study of shopping?
Buy-ology.

When is a shop like a boat?
When it has sales.

Why did the shopkeeper have bells on
his scales?
So they would jingle all the weigh.

MARY: What are you going to
give your little brother for
Christmas?
CARY: I don't know. Last
Christmas I gave him measles.

CUSTOMER: I'm looking for a
present for my mother-in-law
– something cheap and nasty.
SALESGIRL: I've got just the
thing – my father-in-law.

71

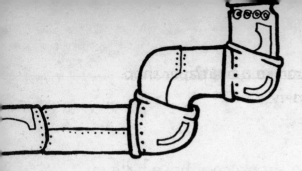

Why didn't the girl want to work in the
clothing factory?
She was too young to dye.

MINNIE: Did you meet your brother at the
supermarket?
WINNIE: Oh no, I've known him for years.

ZIG: How do you make money?
ZAG: Crumple a £5 note and you will find it
in creases.

ZIG: My uncle used to run a paper shop.
ZAG: What happened to it?
ZIG: It blew away.

BOY IN SWEETSHOP: Who's serving the nuts?
ASSISTANT: I'll see to you in a minute.

What did the toothpaste say to the brush?
'Give me a squeeze and I'll meet you outside
the tube.'

Zig went shopping one day and bought an electric blanket. The trouble is, he plugged it into the toaster by mistake, and spent the whole night popping out of bed.

Where do Eskimos keep their money?
In snow banks.

Zig and Zag were trying to decide what to buy for dinner. 'Do you like duck?' asked Zig. 'Yes,' said Zag. 'It's my favourite chicken after turkey.'

Did you hear about the woman who went shopping for 'a dress to wear around the house'? The sales assistant said they hadn't any dresses that big.

FREDA: Mum, I'm going to go out and buy you a pretty china bowl for your birthday.

MUM: Sweet of you, dear, but I've got one.

FREDA: No you haven't, I just dropped it.

ZIG: How many bells are there in the church belfry?

ZAG: About six, all tolled.

What's a popular perfume called?
A best smeller.

Who drives all his customers away?
A taxi driver.

ZIG: There's a book here called *How to Make a Million* but half its pages are missing.
ZAG: Isn't half a million enough for you?

MR WEIRDNOSE: Half a kilo of kiddles, please.
BUTCHER: Do you mean half a kilo of kidneys?
MR WEIRDNOSE: That's what I said, diddle I?

LETTIE: I'm told your boyfriend bought you a necklace from a famous millionaire.
HETTIE: That's right, Woolworth.

78

SHOP ASSISTANT: Last week in our self-service store a man served himself to the till and a pair of trousers.
FRIEND: Did you chase after him?
SHOP ASSISTANT: No, they were my trousers.

79

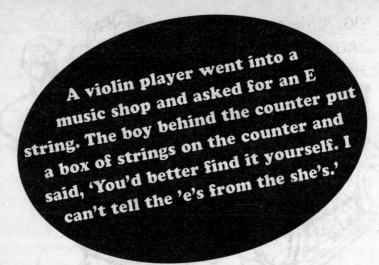

A violin player went into a music shop and asked for an E string. The boy behind the counter put a box of strings on the counter and said, 'You'd better find it yourself. I can't tell the 'e's from the she's.'

Did you hear about the locksmith who was found in a jeweller's shop in the middle of the night?
He told the police he was making a bolt for the door.

How many pineapples can you put in an empty shopping bag?
Just one – after that it isn't empty any more.

ZIG: A friend of mine once opened a shop.
ZAG: How's he doing?
ZIG: Eighteen months. He opened it with a jemmy.

What can a whole apple do that half an apple can't do?
Look round.

LA TRENDY
BOOT SHOP

82

Mr Andy Mann took his small son with him to buy some timber. 'What are all those holes in the planks?' asked the little boy. 'They're knot holes,' explained his father. 'What do you mean they're not holes? I can poke my finger through them.'

What's yellow, weighs a ton, has four legs and sits in a pet shop singing? Two half-ton canaries.

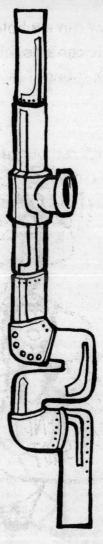

83

What's green, hairy, carries a shopping bag and goes up and down?
A gooseberry in a department store lift.

What's red outside, green and hairy inside and very crowded?
A bus full of gooseberries.

ZIG: I think I'll go and get a haircut.
ZAG: Which one?

Where do gnomes do their shopping?
British Gnome Stores.

85

Where do sheep do their shopping?
Woolworths.

What would
you buy for a
constipated
canary?
Chirrup of figs.

A man stole some
calendars from a
stationer's shop. He got 12 months.

Why did the elephant visit the luggage
shop?
He was looking for a new trunk.

Why did the burglar steal a parrot?
For a lark.

87

SIGN IN A GROCER'S SHOP:

Will customers please not sit on the bacon slicer as we are getting a little behind in our orders.

What happens to a gooseberry when it goes shopping in the rain?
It gets wet.

CUSTOMER: Do you sell dog's meat?
BUTCHER: Only if they can pay.

89

Why are bananas safe from pickpockets?
They don't have any pockets.

'Good morning, sir. I'm from Littlewoods.'
'Blimey! Have I won the pools?'
'No, I'm afraid we caught your wife
shoplifting.'

What happened to the stupid shoplifter?
He was found squashed under the shop.

HARRY: When I go to the fishmonger's he always shakes my hand.
LARRY: He's hoping to keep it out of the till.

Zig was wearing a particularly lurid shirt. 'Do you like it?' he asked Zag. 'I asked the shopkeeper for one that matched my eyes.'

Did you hear about the worm who wanted to buy a washing-machine?
She thought of going to the sales but she didn't want to mangle with the crowds.

CUSTOMER: I didn't come here to be insulted!
SHOP ASSISTANT: Where do you usually go?

91

Zig and Zag Take a holiday

HOLIDAY HA! HA'S!

Why did Zig carry his raincoat when he went on holiday?
Because it couldn't walk.

What do you call a pop singer who spends all his time in hotels?
Hilton John.

What's a twip?
What a wabbit goes on when it twavels.

Who wrote *Quick and Easy Breakfasts*?
Roland Butter.

Why couldn't the jellyfish swim any more?
Because they'd set.

What do cows have for breakfast when they're on holiday?
Moosli.

What do you call robbers who steal meat from the fridge?
Beefburglars.

What's an ig?
An Eskimo's house without a loo.

What do cats like to read when eating breakfast on holiday?
Mewspapers.

And what do they like to eat for their breakfast?
Mice krispies.

Sherlock Holmes was staying in a hotel room when a tree walked in.
'Elm entry, my dear Watson,' he announced.

What's the difference between an elephant and a tomato?
Have you ever seen an elephant in a salad?

'My wife went to the West Indies on holiday.'
'Jamaica?'
'No, she went of her own free will.'

Zig and Zag were on the boating lake, when they heard the attendant shout, 'Come in no. 9, your time's up.' Zag looked round. 'There are only eight boats,' he called. 'Oh dear,' shouted back the attendant. 'No. 6 must be in trouble.'

How can you tell if an elephant shares your
hotel room?
By the dressing-gown with the great big E
on it hanging on the back of the door.

99

Zig and Zag only had one pair of skis so they decided to share them. 'I'll have them going downhill,' said Zig, 'and you can have them going uphill.'

What's the hardest thing
about learning to skate?
The ice!

What did the buffalo say
to his son when he went off on holiday?
'Bison!'

HOTEL MANAGER: Last year we were
burgled. They took everything except the
soap and towels.
ZIG AND ZAG: The dirty crooks!

How do you make an elephant float?
Put it in a large glass with ice-cream and
lemonade.

On their way to their holiday resort Zig and Zag took their old car into a carwash. 'Can you improve its looks?' asked Zig.
'Sorry, sir,' replied the attendant. 'We only wash cars here, we don't iron them as well.'

How do you make an elephant tea?
Well, you start with a very large kettle.

Why were the authorities worried when they saw the elephants on the beach?
In case they dropped their trunks.

103

Why couldn't the elephant travel on the
model railway?
Because his trunk wouldn't fit on the
luggage rack.

104

ZIG: What's the difference between an elephant and a letterbox?
ZAG: I don't know.
ZIG: Well, I shan't ask you to post my postcards then.

Why does an elephant on holiday wear sunglasses?
So no one recognizes him.

ZIG: Have you ever seen a catfish?
ZAG: Yes.
ZIG: How did it hold the rod?

What's the difference between the sea and an elephant?
They're both blue except for the elephant.

ZIG: I used to wear a flower in my lapel but I had to stop.
ZAG: Why?
ZIG: The pot kept hitting me in the stomach.

'Waiter! This food isn't fit for a pig!'
'Hang on, sir, and I'll bring you some that is.'

ZIG: I love sunbathing, don't you.
ZAG: Oh yes. I could sit in the sun all day
and all night.

107

An elephant went to the café on the pier and ordered a strawberry ice-cream. When he came to pay the bill, he handed the cashier a £10 note. Thinking the animal would know nothing about money, the cashier only gave him £1 change. 'We don't get many elephants in here,' the cashier remarked conversationally.

'With ice-creams at £9 each I'm not surprised,' replied the elephant.

108

What do you call a man with a beach on his head?
Sandy.

What do you do if you see a
man with a beach on his head?
Wave!

BEN: We had bad-
tempered pudding
yesterday.
KEN: What's that?
BEN: Apple grumble.

ZIG: When I went to China
I saw a cow hanging from
a tree.
ZAG: Shanghai?
ZIG: No, only about a
metre from the ground.

What's tall, hairy, has a hump and a spends its holidays skiing in Switzerland?
A schizophrenic camel.

What goes right up to a hotel but never goes in?
The drive.

'Waiter! I can't eat this food! It's disgusting! Fetch the manager!'
'It's no use, sir, he won't eat it either.'

'Waiter! What's this fly doing on my ice-cream?'
'Learning to ski, sir.'

ZIG: You'll have to behave properly if we stay in this hotel. Remember, take off your shoes before you put your feet on the table.

111

Why did the monster who ate windows feel ill?
Because he had a pane in his stomach.

What do you call a cat that's eaten a duck?
A duck-filled fatty puss.

What's grey, has four legs and a trunk?
A mouse going on holiday.

113

Why did the elephant sleep under the bed?
Because he thought he was a little potty.

What's grey, has four legs and two trunks?
A mouse emigrating.

POLICEMAN: Why did you park here?
MOTORIST: Because the notice says 'Fine for parking'.

114

What makes mountain climbers so curious?
They always want to take another peak.

115

Did you hear about the boy scout whose beret blew off when he was camping in a field full of cows? He had to try on 20 before he found it!

What did Paddington and Winnie the Pooh take on holiday?
Just the bear essentials.

Zig and Zag were unpacking. 'That's a strange pair of socks, Zig,' said Zag. 'One's yellow and green, the other's red and blue.'
'Yes,' said Zig. 'And I've got another pair just the same at home.'

Where do cruise passengers hold parties on board ship?
Where the funnel be.

Where did the pig go on holiday?
To visit his pen-pal.

ZIG: The gravy's always lumpy in this hotel.
ZAG: That's a bad sign.
ZIG: What's it a sign of?
ZAG: It's a sign the chef has a cold!

Zig and Zag's Olympic Games

OLYMPIC GIGGLES!

Can you swim on a full stomach?
Yes, but it's easier in water.

How do you start a jelly race?
You say, 'Get set!'

How do you start a rice pudding race?
Sago!

What do boxers like reading?
Scrap books.

The young man learning to box was not very
good. 'Never mind, lad,' said his coach. 'Just
keep swinging, the draught might give your
opponent a cold.'

Why did a party of opticians go to the
Olympic Games?
Because it was such a spectacle.

121

ZIG: What made you decide to take up parachuting?
ZAG: A plane with engine failure.

Why is a football stadium so cool? Because there's a fan on every seat.

FLYING INSTRUCTOR: Tomorrow you can fly solo.
ZIG: How low?

ZIG: I went fly-fishing last week.
ZAG: Catch anything?
ZIG: Yes, a five-pound bluebottle.

When a team of elephants played football with a team of ants one elephant squashed an ant and was sent off the field. 'But I didn't mean to tread on him,' said the elephant sadly. 'I only meant to trip him up.'

124

Why is it that every time the doorbell rings, my dog goes into a corner?
He's a boxer.

Why couldn't the idiot play water polo?
He couldn't get his horses into the
swimming pool.

Why did the rich idiot have two swimming
pools – one without any water in it?
The empty one was for people who
couldn't swim.

ZIG: Why can't you swim in a small pool full of green, slimy water?
ZAG: Because it's snot for swimming in.

What has 22 legs and two wings but can't fly?
A football team.

ZAG: *Why was Cinderella no good at football?*
ZIG: *I don't know. Why was Cinderella no good at football?*
ZAG: *Because her coach was a pumpkin.*

129

ZIG: Why else was Cinderella no good at football?
ZAG: I don't know. Why else was Cinderella no good at football?
ZIG: Because she kept running away from the ball!

Which athlete keeps warmest in winter? The long jumper.

ZIG: I can jump higher than a house.
ZAG: Don't be daft.
ZIG: I can. A house can't jump!

How can you swim 100 metres in five seconds?
Over a waterfall.

ZAG: In Australia we chased kangaroos on horses.
ZIG: Really? I didn't know kangaroos could ride horses.

What happens to old horses?
They become nags.

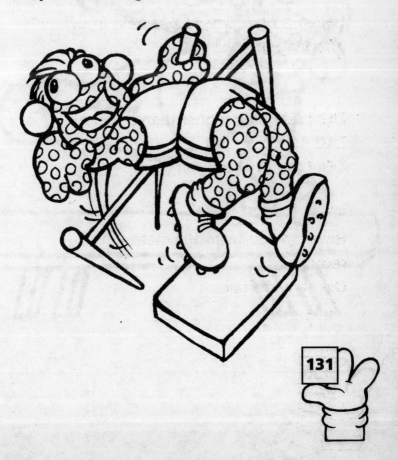

What's the hardest thing about learning to ride a horse?
The ground.

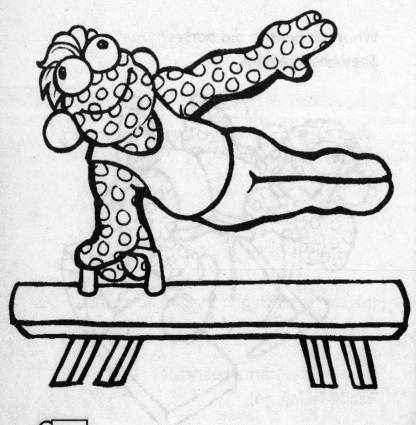

What's red and white, plays football and
sits in a corner of the kitchen?
A fridge draped in a football scarf.
(I lied about it playing football!)

What's a horse's favourite game?
Stable tennis.

What were the elephants playing in the
broom cupboard?
Squash.

Two flies were playing football in a saucer.
One said: 'We'll have to do better than
this, we're playing in the cup next week.'

How do you start a bear race?
Ready, teddy, go!

133

What football team never meets before a match?
Queen's Park Strangers.

Why couldn't Zig sit down for a week when he'd been playing football?
He got a kick in the penalty area.

Who gets the most kicks out of his job?
A footballer.

What position did the ghost have in the football team?

Why is tennis such a noisy game?
Because everyone raises a racket.

What do people serve, but no one eats?
Tennis balls.

135

Did you hear that a group of football referees are going to make a film? They're calling it *The Umpire Strikes Back*.

ZIG: *If you have referees in football and umpires in cricket, what do you have in bowls?*
ZAG: *Goldfish?*

'You'd be a good footballer if it weren't for two things.'
'What are they?'
'Your feet!'

'What position do you play in the football team?'
'I think I'm one of the drawbacks.'

Zig and Zag Go to the Seaside

SEASIDE

SILLIES!

What's big, green and swims in
the sea?
An unripe sea monster.

What's the best day to go to the beach?
Sun-day.

Why is it impossible to starve on a beach?
Because of the sand which is there.

What did the sea say to the shore?
Nothing, it just waved.

What did the grape say when the
elephant trod on it?
Nothing, it let out a little wine.

140

Why did the lobster blush?
Because the seaweed.

What sits at the bottom of the sea and shivers?
A nervous wreck.

ZIG: You remind me of the sea.
ZAG: Because I'm wild, untamed and romantic?
ZIG: No, because you make me sick.

What do fish in the sea sing at Christmas?
'Shark, the herald angels sing.'

What did one rock pool say
to another?
'Show us your mussels.'

Why was the diver embarrassed?
Because he saw the ship's bare bottom.

What's black, floats on water and shouts,
'Knickers!'
Crude oil.

What's black, floats on water and
shouts, 'Underwear!'
Refined oil.

143

What did the octopus buy her husband for Christmas?
Four pairs of socks.

What fish only swims at night?
A starfish.

What does a deaf fisherman wear?
A herring aid.

ZIG: How can you stop fish from smelling?
ZAG: Cut off their noses.

144

What's round, leaf-green and
smells fishy?
Brussels sprats.

What fish can perform operations?
A sturgeon.

When is a boat like a fall of snow?
When it's adrift.

BEN: My sister's a bathing beauty.
KEN: I'd heard she was a girl worth wading for.

What seabird is always out of breath?
A puffin.

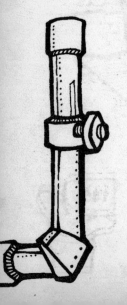

Knock, knock.
Who's there?
Michelle.
Michelle who?
Michelle had a crab inside it.

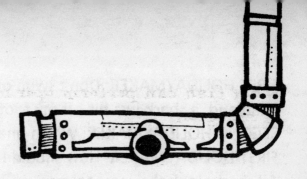

Why did the ocean roar?
It had crabs all over its bottom.

Which fish terrorizes other fish?
Jack the Kipper.

What do you call a neurotic octopus?
A crazy, mixed-up squid.

Zig said to Zag, 'Can you lend me 10p?
I need to phone a friend.'
Zag replied, 'Here's 20p, phone all your
friends.'

FIRST HOLIDAYMAKER: Don't swim off that headland, a shark just bit off my foot.
SECOND HOLIDAYMAKER: Which one?
FIRST HOLIDAYMAKER: How should I know? All sharks look the same to me.

Where do you weigh a whale?
At a whale-weigh station.

ZIG: I'm on a seafood diet.
ZAG: You don't look any slimmer to me.
ZIG: No, every time I see food I eat it.

What did the German boy say as he
pushed his brother over the cliff?
'Look, Mum, no Hans!'

What do you call a baby whale that
cries a lot?
A little blubber.

What swims in the sea with a machine-gun and
makes you an offer you can't refuse?
The Codfather.

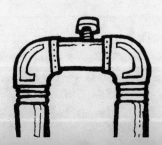

149

'May I have another glass of water?'
'But that's the fourth you've had.'
'I know, but my little sister's still
on fire.'

ZIG: OK. What about the place in the town square? They serve crabs.
ZAG: At the prices they charge I should think they're glad to serve anybody.

How do ghosts cross the Channel?
By hovercraft.

What's brown and comes
steaming out of Cowes?
The Isle of Wight ferry.

What's brown and sounds like a bell?
Dung!

151

ZAG: Shall I recite a poem?

ZIG: If you like.

ZAG: There was a young lady called Nellie,
Who waded in the sea up to her knees . . .

ZIG: That doesn't rhyme.

ZAG: I know, but the water was too cold for
her to go in any deeper.

Why was the little boy locked up on
the ship?
Because he thought the poop deck
was the place to go.

What's the difference between a lavatory
brush and a ginger biscuit?
You can't dunk a lavatory brush in your tea.

What happened when Ray fell over
the cliff?
He became X-ray.

What kind of sea creature eats its victims
two by two?
Noah's shark.

153

What fish tastes better with cream?
A jellyfish.

154

What do you call a man with a seagull
on his head?
Cliff.

How do the police chase criminals in the sea?
With a squid car.

What has 12 legs, six ears and a bad smell
and one eye?
Three blind mice and half a rotten fish.

When does a bee fly
with its back legs
crossed?
When it's looking
for a BP station.

What did one sardine say to another when it saw a submarine?
'There goes a tin full of people.'

What is sandpaper?
A map of the beach.

What swims along the seabed and gets trodden on?
A wall-to-wall carp.

Zig and Zag were on a cruise when the weather got very rough, and a steward came along and found them groaning on the deck.
'Shall I serve you supper in your cabin?' he asked.
'No thanks,' said Zig and Zag. 'Just throw it overboard to save us doing it later.'

What's the best cure for seasickness?
Bolt your food down.

157

ZIG, ON SHIP: I've put all my clothes in that cupboard with the little round window.

Why could Zag never join the
submarine service?
Because he likes sleeping with the
windows open.

What do you call the ghost of a sailor?
A sea ghoul.

What's green, hairy and zooms
across the bay at 40 km per hour?
A gooseberry with an outboard
motor.

159

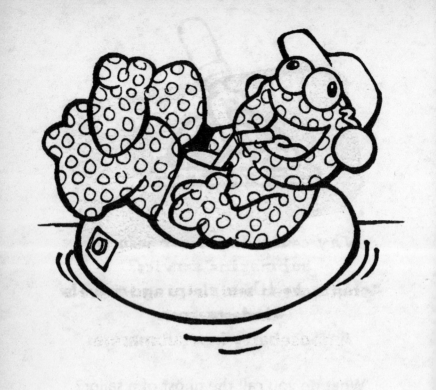

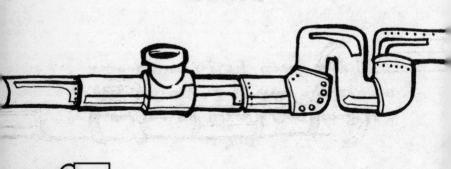

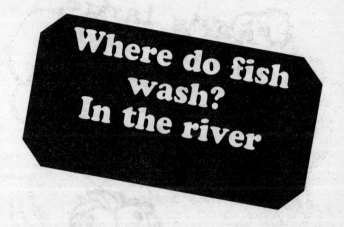

Where do fish wash? In the river

What's green and hairy and travels underwater?
A gooseberry in a submarine.

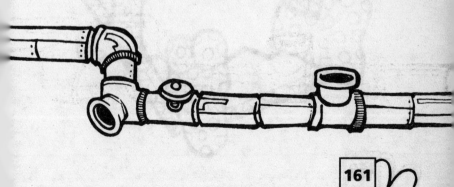

What's large,
purple and
surrounded by
sea?
Grape Britain.

162

What kind of a
ship was Dracula
captain of?
A blood vessel.

When is a sailor not a sailor?
When he's aboard.

164

What do you call bad-tempered dolphins?
Cross porpoises.

What did Noah say to his sons as they were fishing over the side of the ark?
'Take it easy, boys, remember I only have two worms.'

What's a phantom navy called?
The ghost guard.

What do you give a sick sea monster?
Plenty of room.

What do you use to cut through giant
waves?
A sea-saw.

Two seagulls were
flying over a smart
car showroom. One
said *to the other*, 'Let's
put a deposit on a
Ferrari.'

What do you get if you cross the Atlantic with the *Titanic*? Halfway.

What sea creature is good at maths? An octoplus.

ZIG: Why did you give me a lobster with only one claw?
WAITER: Sorry, sir, it must have been in a fight.
ZIG: Then take it away and bring me the winner.

Why was the crab arrested?
Because it kept pinching things.

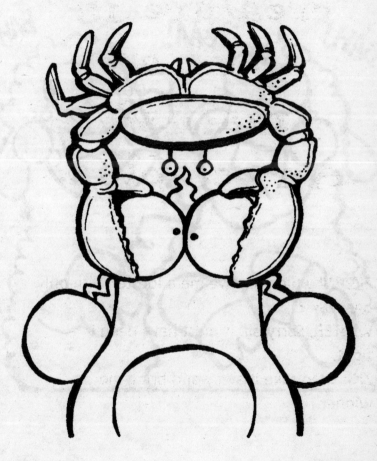

ZIG AND ZAG ON THE FARM

FARMYARD FUNNIES!

What do you get from a frightened cow?
Milk shakes.

**WHAT DO YOU GET IF YOU CROSS A
CAMEL WITH A COW?
LUMPY MILK SHAKES.**

Where do all good chickens go when they die?
To oven.

ZIG: Why did the punk cross the road?
ZAG: Because he was stapled to the chicken.

**WHO TELLS CHICKEN JOKES?
COMEDI-HENS.**

ZAG: Whatever happens, Zig, don't walk under a cow.

ZIG: Why not?

ZAG: You might get a pat on the head.

HOW DO BABY HENS DANCE? CHICK TO CHICK.

Why is it a waste of time holding a party for chickens?
Because it's hard to make hens meet.

What did one pig say to the other?
'Let's be pen pals.'

174

What's streaky bacon.
A pig running round without its clothes on.

What do you call a stupid pig thief?
A hamburglar.

What do you call high-rise housing for pigs?
Styscrapers.

Why wouldn't the piglets listen to their father?
Because he was such an old boar.

WHAT DO FEMALE SHEEP WEAR? EWENIFORMS.

FIRST SHEEP: Baaa.
SECOND SHEEP: Moo.
FIRST SHEEP: What do you mean, 'moo'?
SECOND SHEEP: I'm learning a foreign language.

WHAT DO YOU GET IF YOU CROSS A SHEEP WITH A THUNDERSTORM? A WET BLANKET.

A goat was eating a can of film on a rubbish tip. His friend asked if it was any good. 'Not bad,' replied the first goat, 'but I preferred the book.'

WHAT DO YOU GET IF YOU CROSS A HEN WITH AN ELECTRIC ORGAN? HAMMOND EGGS.

Why is it difficult to hold a
conversation with a goat?
It always butts in.

177

What's soft, yellow and goes round
and round?
A long-playing omelette.

What do you call a mischievous egg?
A practical yolker.

WHAT DO YOU GET IF YOU CROSS A TRACTOR WITH A DOG? A LAND ROVER.

What do you get if you cross a sheepdog with a vegetable?
A collie-flower.

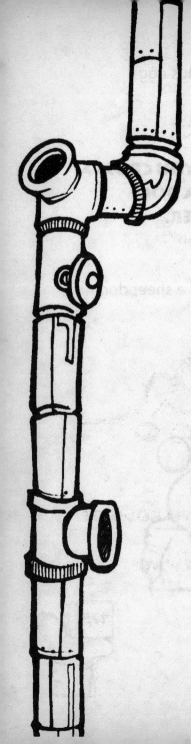

Who wrote *Organic Farming*?
Rosa Carrots.

What's a hen's favourite TV programme?
The feather forecast.

What's green and goes boing, boing?
Spring cabbage.

ZIG AND ZAG: What's the farm cat called?
YOUNG LAD: Ben Hur.
ZIG AND ZAG: That's an odd name for a cat.
YOUNG LAD: It was just call Ben until it had kittens.

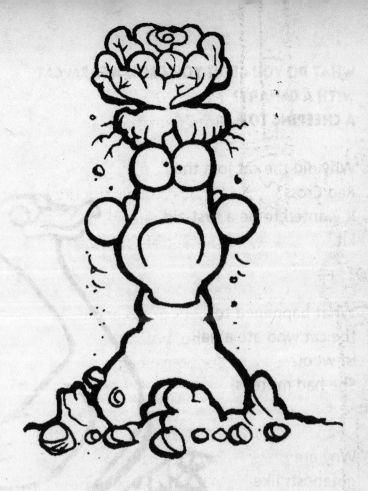

WHAT DO YOU CALL TWO ROWS OF CABBAGES? A DUAL CABBAGEWAY.

WHAT DO YOU GET IF YOU CROSS A FARM CAT WITH A CANARY? A CHEEPING TOM.

Why did the cat join the Red Cross? It wanted to be a first-aid kit.

What happened to the cat who ate a ball of wool? She had mittens.

Why are gateposts like seeds? Because they propagate.

182

What do you call films made about farmyard birds?
Duckumentaries.

ZAG: Which of these ducks' feathers can you use to stuff a quilt?
ZIG: Eider.

ZIG: What happens to a duck before it grows up?
ZAG: It grows down!

**WHAT DO YOU GET IF YOU CROSS A COCKEREL WITH A POODLE?
A COCKERPOODLEDO!**

FIRST FARMER: The man who stole my prize pig is in gaol.
SECOND FARMER: How was he caught?
FIRST FARMER: The pig squealed.

What do you do with a sick pig?
Take it to hospital in a hambulance and give it oinkment.

ZIG: What happened to that friend of yours, Mucky Martin?
ZAG: He's doing farmyard impressions now.
ZIG: What does he do, animal noises?
ZAG: No, he does the smells.

How many pigs does it take to make a stink?
A phew.

WHAT DO YOU GIVE A SICK RABBIT? A HOPERATION.

How do you catch a rabbit?
Hide behind a tree and make a noise like a lettuce.

WHAT HAPPENS IF YOU POUR BOILING WATER DOWN A RABBIT HOLE? YOU GET HOT CROSS BUNNIES.

What did the dog say when he sat on the sandpaper?
'Ruff.'

What goes 'tock, tock, woof?'
A watchdog.

Why do cows have bells?
Because their horns don't work.

Why do cows lie down when it rains?
To keep each udder warm.

**WHY ARE FARMERS OFTEN SMELLY?
THEY WEAR DUNG-AREES.**

What's red, has 12 legs and runs round a field?
Three cows wearing tracksuits.

188

What do you call a bee born in May?
A maybe.

What wakes hens in the
morning?
An alarm cluck.

How do you count cows?
With a cowculator.

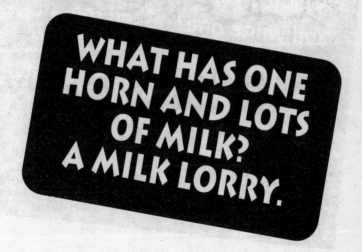

WHAT HAS ONE
HORN AND LOTS
OF MILK?
A MILK LORRY.

189

A man was driving down a country lane when his car broke down, and a cow looking over the hedge suggested he check the petrol tank. Astonished, he ran up the lane to the farmhouse and told the farmer. 'Was it a Hereford cow – a red and white one?' asked the farmer.

'That's right,' said the motorist.

'Then don't take any notice of her. Herefords don't know a thing about cars.'

190

What did one horse say to the other?
'I don't remember your face, but your mane is familiar.'

**HOW MANY COWS DOES IT TAKE TO CHANGE A LIGHT BULB?
DON'T BE SILLY, COWS CAN'T CHANGE LIGHT BULBS.**

What's a cow's favourite entertainment?
A night at the moovies.

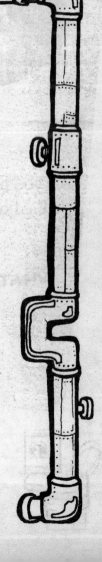

What's streaky bacon? A pig running about without clothes on.

Did you hear about Wild Bill McAbe?
He died of mad cowboy disease.

**WHAT KIND OF COW DO YOU KEEP
IN A GARDEN SHED?
A LAWN MOOER.**

How did the sheep feel when it
swallowed a cow?
Very ba-a-a-a-a-d.

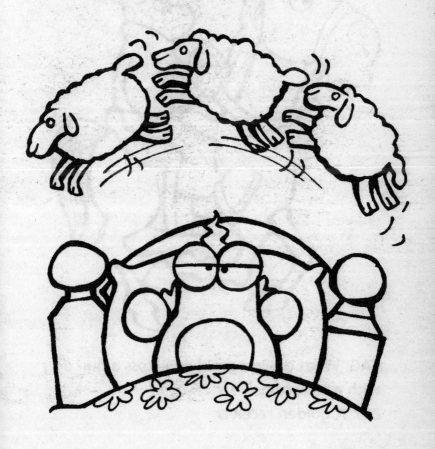

ZAG: What do you get if you cross a gun dog with a telephone?
ZIG: A golden receiver.

194

ZIG: Some cows were walking down towards the milking shed. There was a cow in front of two cows, a cow behind two cows, and a cow between two cows. How many cows were there altogether?

I don't know, I can't add up that many.

ZIG: Three.

(Think about it!)

What do you get if you cross a mongrel dog with a muddy farm track?

A mutt in a rut.

What do you get if you cross an elephant with a chicken?
A very messy henhouse.

What games do calves play at parties?
Moosical chairs.

WHAT HAPPENED TO THE COW ONE VERY COLD WINTER?
SHE PRODUCED ICE-CREAM!

WHAT ANIMAL HAS TWO HUMPS AND IS FOUND AT THE NORTH POLE? A LOST CAMEL.

197

What's green, curved and goes slam, slam, slam?
A cucumber hatchback.

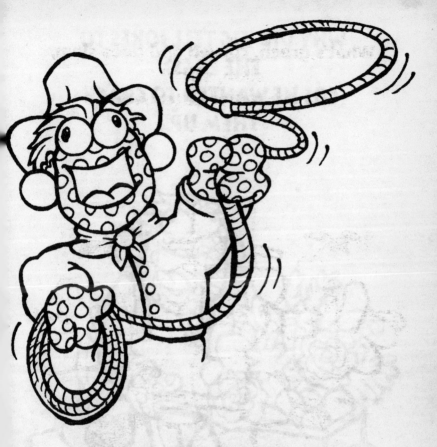

**WHAT DO YOU GET WHEN YOU
CROSS A COW, A SHEEP AND A
YOUNG GOAT?
THE MILKY BAA KID.**

199

WHY DID ZIG TELL JOKES TO THE EGGS? 'COS HE WANTED TO CRACK THEM UP.

What's the difference between a plane and a tree?
One leaves its shed and the other sheds its leaves.

WHERE DO YOU TAKE A SICK HORSE?
HORSEPITAL.

WHAT DO YOU GIVE A PONY WITH A COLD?
COUGH STIRRUP.

SPELL A HUNGRY HORSE IN FOUR LETTERS.
M.T.G.G.

Which side of a chicken is most feathery?
The outside.

ZIG: I've just bought a pig.
ZAG: Where will you keep it?
ZIG: In my bedroom.
ZAG: But what about the smell?
ZIG: Oh, the pig won't mind that.

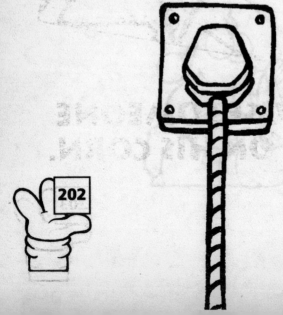

WHY WAS THE FARMER CROSS?

BECAUSE SOMEONE TROD ON HIS CORN.

203

WHAT DID THE BULL SAY TO THE COW? WHEN I FALL IN LOVE IT WILL BE FOR HEIFER.

204

HOW DOES A SHEEP KEEP WARM IN WINTER? BY CENTRAL BLEATING.

205

ZIG AND ZAG'S HORROR MOVIE

HILARIOUS HORRORS!

ZIG: Can you tell me how to join the Dracula Fan Club?
ZAG: Yes, send them your name, address and blood group.

FIRST MONSTER: That girl over there rolled her eyes at me.
SECOND MONSTER: Well, roll them back, she might need them.

HOW DOES A MONSTER COUNT UP TO 13? ON ITS FINGERS.

What space film is about Dracula?
The Vampire Strikes Back.

HETTIE: My boyfriend took me to see *Land of the Monster* at the cinema last night.

LETTIE: Scary?

HETTIE: Yes, about eight feet tall, hairy, with bloodshot eyes and long fangs.

LETTIE: Not your boyfriend, what was the film like?

WHAT DO VAMPIRES HAVE AT 10.30 EVERY MORNING? A COFFIN BREAK.

What goes chomp, suck, ouch!
A vampire with toothache.

ZIG: What's a skeleton?
ZAG: I don't know. What's a skeleton?
ZIG: Bones with people scraped off.

Why didn't the skeleton go parachute jumping?
Because he didn't have the guts.

'Mummy, Mummy, I don't like Daddy!'
'Well, leave him at the side of your plate and just eat your chips.'

'MUMMY, MUMMY, DADDY'S GOING OUT!' 'HERE'S ANOTHER MATCH, SET FIRE TO HIM AGAIN!'

ZAG: What do short-sighted ghosts wear?
ZIG: Spooktacles.
Where do ghosts go swimming?
In the Dead Sea.

WHAT DO ITALIAN GHOSTS EAT FOR DINNER? SPOOKHETTI.

The ghost teacher was explaining to her class how to walk through locked doors. 'Did you all understand?' she asked. 'If not I'll go through it again.'

What did one ghost say to another?
'I don't care what you say, I'll never believe in people.'

214

HOW DOES A GHOST BEGIN
A LETTER?
TOMB IT MAY CONCERN . . .'

What's a ghost boxer called?
A phantomweight.

Why was the ghost arrested when he was carrying a gun?
Because he didn't have a haunting licence.

What happened when the skeleton went to a party?
People kept hanging their coats on him.

ZIG: Why don't you go out and play football with your brother?
ZAG: Because it's easier with a ball.

MICKEY MONSTER: Mum, why do I keep going round in circles?
MOTHER MONSTER: Shut up, or I'll nail your other foot to the floor.

How do you greet a three-headed monster?
'Hello, hello, hello!'

What card game did the monster play with
the crocodile?
Snap.

Knock, knock.
Who's there?
Hugo.
Hugo who?
Hugo first into
the haunted
house!

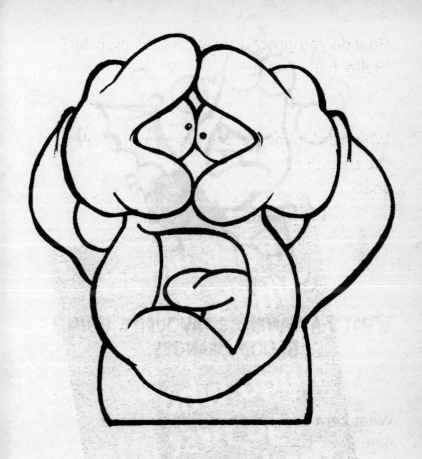

'I HATE MY SISTER'S GUTS.'
'BE QUIET AND EAT WHAT YOU'RE
GIVEN

WHAT'S A VAMPIRE'S FAVOURITE FRUIT?
BLOOD ORANGES.

What kept the vampire's wife awake at night?
His coffin.

ZIG: What do green-eyed hairy-footed
monsters have that no one else has?
ZAG: Baby green-eyed hairy-footed monsters.

HOW DID THE WEREWOLF SIGN
HIS LETTERS?
'BEST VICIOUS.'

Who wrote a book about werewolves?
Norah Bone.
FIRST WITCH: Why is your toad going 'dit, dit, dit, dot, dot'?
SECOND WITCH: He's a morse toad.

ZIG: What kind of monster lives in your nose?
ZAG: A bogeyman.

Knock, knock.
Who's there?
Fred.
Fred who?
Fred of ghosts, are you?

HOW CAN YOU HELP A STARVING CANNIBAL? GIVE HIM A HAND.

HOW DOES THE ABOMINABLE SNOWMAN TRAVEL AROUND? BY ICICLE.

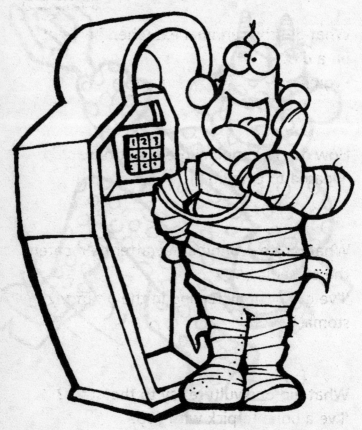

What did the vegetarian
cannibal eat?
Swedes.

What did the cannibal eat when he went
on a diet?
Pygmies.

How does a cannibal greet a stranger?
'Pleased to eat you.'

What did the cannibal say after he'd eaten
the comedian?
'I've got a funny feeling in the pit of my
stomach.'

What did one vulture say to the other?
'I've a bone to pick with you.'

Why was Dr Frankenstein never lonely?
He was good at making friends.

WHAT DO ZOMBIES LIKE WITH THEIR BREAD AND CHEESE? PICKLED ORGANS.

What's a vampire's favourite soup?
Scream of tomato.

BARBER: Sorry, sir, my hand slipped and I've cut your neck.
DRACULA: That's all right. It's not *my* blood.

227

WHAT'S A VAMPIRE'S FAVOURITE
BREAKFAST CEREAL?
READY NECK.

228

What screams more loudly than Zig
frightened by a horror film?
Zig and Zag frightened by a horror film.

What did the vampire say when he'd finished
with his victim?
'Fangs very much.'

WHAT KIND OF SANDALS DO WITCHES WEAR? OPEN-TOAD.

What do you call a nervous sorceress?
A twitch.

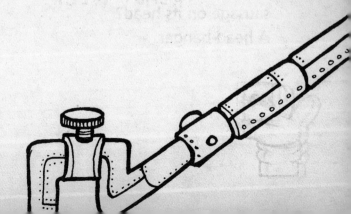

WHY ARE VAMPIRES THIN? THEY EAT NECKS TO NOTHING.

What do you call a ghost with a spade on its head?
Doug.

What do you call a ghost with a sausage on its head?
A head-banger.

HOW DO GHOULS CELEBRATE?
THEY PAINT THE TOWN DEAD.

What do you call a mummy who eats biscuits in bed?
A crumby mummy.

**What's the difference between a musician and a corpse?
One composes, the other decomposes.**

**Where does the ghost of
Pocahontas live?
In a creepy tepee.**

KNOCK, KNOCK.
WHO'S THERE?
IVAN.
IVAN WHO?
IVAN TO DRINK YOUR BLOOD.

233

FIRST CANNIBAL: Am I too late for dinner?

SECOND CANNIBAL: Yes, I'm afraid everybody's eaten.

YOUNG CANNIBAL: I'VE BROUGHT A FRIEND HOME FOR TEA, MUM.

MOTHER CANNIBAL: THAT'S NICE, DEAR. WE'LL PUT HIM IN THE LARDER AND EAT HIM NEXT WEEK.

FIRST MONSTER: Is your girlfriend pretty or ugly?
SECOND MONSTER: I'd say she was pretty ugly.

235

ZIG: WHAT HAPPENED WHEN
THE BOY GHOST MET THE GIRL
GHOST?
ZAG: THEY FELL IN LOVE AT
FIRST FRIGHT.

236

What goes ha, ha, ha, thump?
A monster laughing its head off.

WHAT DO YOU GET IF YOU CROSS THE ABOMINABLE SNOWMAN AND A SHARK? FROSTBITE.

What do you call a play that's acted by ghosts?
A phantomime.

WHAT DO GHOSTS EAT FOR LUNCH? GHOULASH.

237

WHAT WALKS BACKWARDS THROUGH WALLS GOING, 'ER . . . BOO'? A NERVOUS GHOST.

What do you get if you cross a ghost and a
packet of crisps?
Snacks that go munch in the night.
How does a witch tell the time?
She wears a witch watch.

WHAT'S DRACULA'S FAVOURITE SONG? FANGS FOR THE MEMORY'.

Where does Dracula get all his jokes?
From his crypt writer.

ZAG: Did Dracula have a wife?
ZIG: No, he was a bat-chelor?

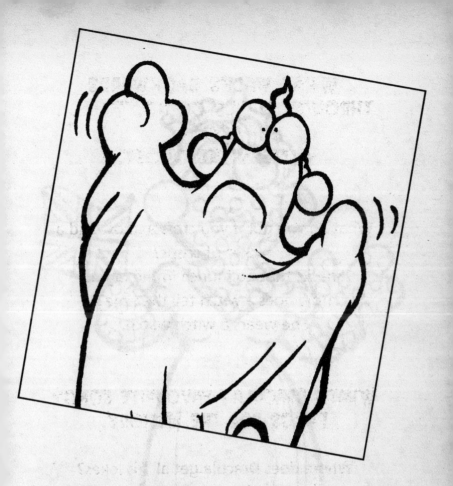

NASTY SISTER: DON'T LOOK OUT OF THE WINDOW, SUSIE, PEOPLE WILL THINK IT'S HALLOWE'EN.

239

Zig and Zag Go Round the World

WORLD-WIDE WOBBLERS!

ZIG: How far is Buckingham Palace from Westminster Abbey?
ZAG: About 15 minutes' walk if you run.

While Zig and Zag were in London they met a man carrying a violin case who asked them the way to the Albert Hall.
'Practice,' replied Zig.

PASSENGER: How long will the next train be?
GUARD: About six carriages.

Where in London are drivers especially noisy?
Tooting.

What's made from custard and jelly, stands in the middle of Paris and wobbles? The Trifle Tower.

243

FIRST ROMAN: What's the time?
SECOND ROMAN: XX past VI.

Why did the Romans build straight roads?
So their soldiers wouldn't go round the bend.

ZAG: What was the Romans' greatest
achievement?
ZIG: Learning Latin!

ZIG AND ZAG: Will our pizzas be long?
WAITER: No, round, like everyone else's.

DINER: Have you got frogs' legs?
WAITER: No, it's just the way I walk.

Who makes spaghetti bombs?
The Minestrone of Defence.

How do you make a Swiss roll?
Push him down a mountain.

ZIG: How do you make a Venetian blind?
ZAG: Stick your finger in his eye.

ZAG: What's a Grecian urn?
ZIG: About 50 drachmas a week.

Why was Zig and Zag's frying pan like a museum?
It was full of ancient grease.

ZIG: I went to Switzerland once.
ZAG: Did you like the scenery?
ZIG: I couldn't see much of it. There were too many mountains in the way.

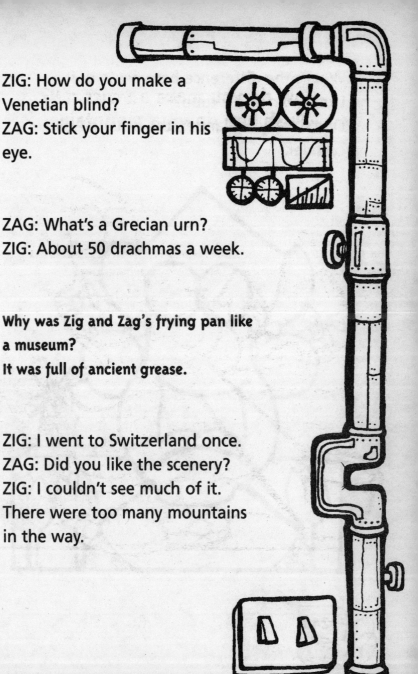

What's the difference between a daft Dutchman and a tube?
One's a silly Hollander, the other a hollow cylinder.

248

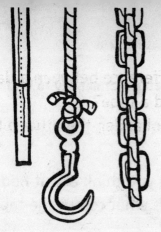

**What did the Dutchman who kept a
pet shop have for tea?
'Amster jam.**

What do you call a very small man who
works on the Paris Underground?
A Metro gnome.

**How did the Vikings communicate
with one another?
By Norse code.**

What did the Spanish farmer say to his hens?
'Olé!'

ZAG: What do you think about Red China?
ZIG: It depends what colour the tablecloth is.

What did Zig say to his German barber?
'Good morning, Herr Dresser.'

Where are motor horns made?
Hong King.

What's purple and thousands of miles long?
The Grape Wall of China.

Who ruled over a vast empire of cats
in the East?
Chairman Miaow.

250

What did the ancient Chinese wear in winter to keep warm?
Ming coats.

What kind of jokes did Socrates make?
Wisecracks.

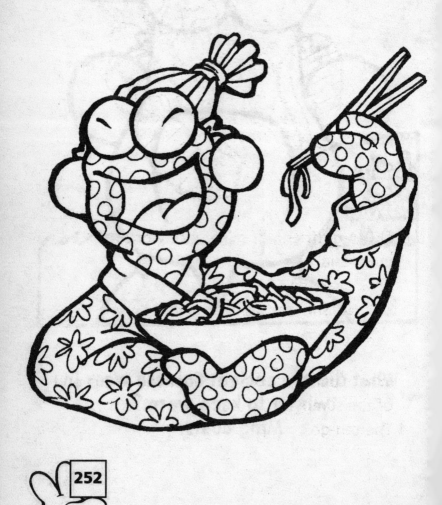

ZIG: A girlfriend of mine once went to
Indonesia.
ZAG: Djakarta?
ZIG: No, she went on her own.

What Spanish dance do people do at the end
of the summer?
The tan-go.

253

Who rides a camel and carries a lamp?
Florence of Arabia.

What did one Turk say to the other?
'I don't remember your name, but your fez is
familiar.'

What do you call a camel with three humps?
Humphrey!

What did Zig and Zag
take when they visited
the Sahara?
A thirst-aid kit.

Why did the egg go into the jungle?
It was an egg-splorer.

How do monkeys toast bread?
They put it under the g'rilla.

When is a monkey like a flower?
When it's a chimp-pansy.

ZIG: What do you get if you cross a
crocodile with a rose?
ZAG: I don't know, but I wouldn't try
smelling it!

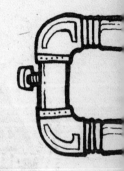

What has a mane and purple feet and
lives in Africa?
A lion that makes its own wine.

Why can't you put an elephant in a sandwich?
It wouldn't fit in your lunchbox.

A man on safari met a lion face to face and fainted. When he recovered he saw the lion on its knees praying, so he said, 'Thank you for not eating me.' 'Shh,' said the lion. 'I'm saying grace.'

**What has two trunks, eight legs and three tails?
An elephant with spare parts.**

What's worse than being a giraffe with a sore throat? Being a giraffe with a stiff neck.

Zig and Zag met a giraffe. 'Why do you have such a long neck?', asked Zig. 'Because my feet smell,' replied the giraffe.

If a giraffe gets its feet wet, does it get a sore throat? Yes, but not for a week or so.

What's large, grey, smelly and might sit
on you?
An elephant's bottom.

Why did the elephant wear a yellow wig?
To see if blondes really do have more fun.

What's large, green and has a trunk?
An unripe elephant.

What jungle animal should you never play
cards with?
A cheetah.

What would you do with a blue elephant?
Try to cheer it up.

263

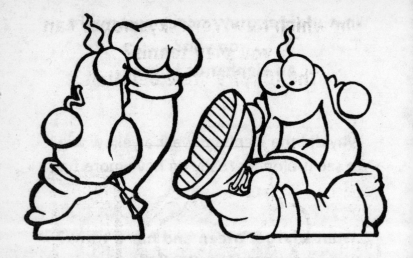

What happened when two kangaroos got married?
They lived hoppily ever after.

Why is the year 2000 good for kangaroos?
Because it's a leap year.

In which New York skyscraper can you play tennis?
The Umpire State Building.

Which native American tribe produced the most lawyers? The Sioux.

What is a small
laugh in
native
American
language?
A minne-haha.

What do you call an American drawing?
A Yankee doodle.

What did Delaware?
A New Jersey.

267

What was the matter with the exhausted
kangaroo?
It was out of bounds.

Knock,
knock.
Who's
there?
Yukon.
Yukon
who?
Yukon go
away and
come back
later.

Who had eight guns and terrorized the ocean?
Billy the Squid.

269

Knock, knock.
Who's there?
Oslo.
Oslo who?
Oslo down, what's the hurry?

Which famous Wild West character suffered
from indigestion?
Wild Bill Hiccup.

ZIG: Why do they call me 'Paleface'?
ZAG: Because you've got a face like a bucket.

Knock, knock.
Who's there?
Indonesia.
Indonesia who.
When I look at you I go weak Indonesia.

'Could you see me across the road,
constable?'
'I could see you from a mile away.'

271

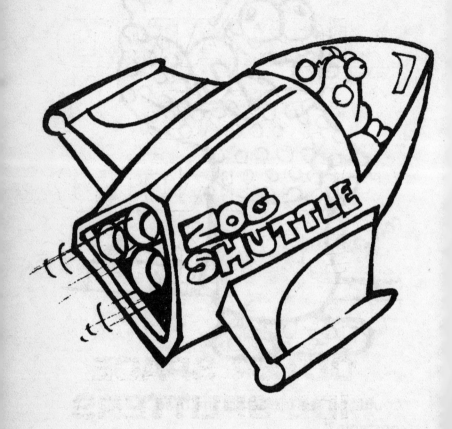

ZIG AND ZAG GO INTO SPACE

OUTER SPACE
SIDE SPLITTERS

What do you call a crazy spaceman?
An astronut.

What do you get if you cross an old misery
with a spaceship?
A moan rocket.

SPACE TRAFFIC
CONTROL: What is
your height and
position?
SPACESHIP PILOT:
I'm 1.75 metres tall
and I'm sitting in the
cockpit.

When Zig and Zag went to the travel agents to ask for two tickets to the moon, the agent said, 'Sorry, gents, the moon's full at the moment.'

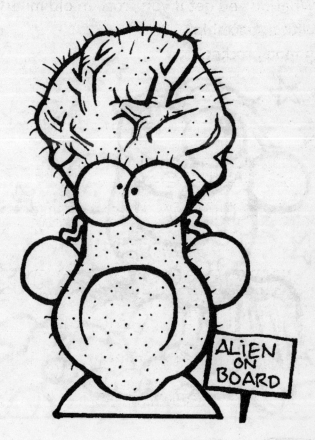

If a spaceship crashed on the border between America and Canada where would the survivors be buried?
Nowhere, because they wouldn't be dead!

What's big, bright and stupid? A fool moon.

When is a window like a star?
When it's a skylight.

PASSENGER: How long is the flight to the Planet Zog?
CLERK: Just a minute . . .
PASSENGER: Thanks very much.

277

Why do the members of a spaceship's crew have to agree? Because they don't want to fall out.

What do Zoggians do with orange peel? Throw it away, of course!

ZIG, ON SPACESHIP: Do these spaceships crash often?
SPACESHIP PILOT: No, only once!

What's furry and wears sunglasses? A Zoggian in disguise.

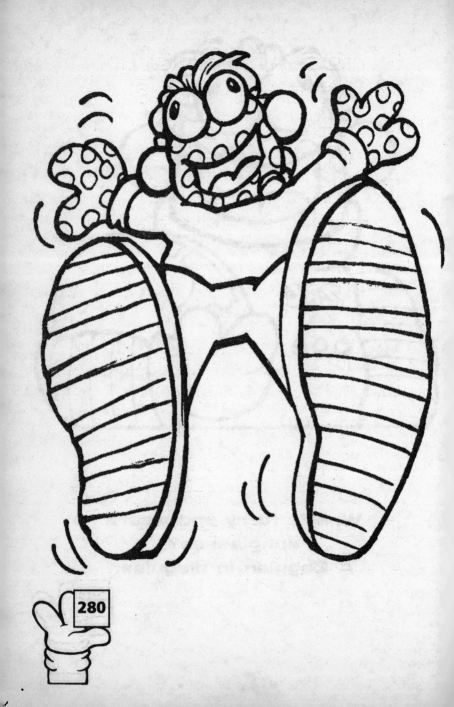

Knock, knock.
Who's there?
Philip.
Philip who?
Philip the tank,
we're off into
space.

Knock, knock.
Who's there?
Venus.
Venus who?
Venus it time to
board the
rocket?

What do rocket pilots hang up at Christmas?
Missile-toe.

Why did the spaceman walk?
Because he'd missed the bus.

What's a space traveller's favourite game?
Astro-noughts and crosses.

What did the star
win in the space
competition?
A constellation
prize.

282

How do you keep flies out of
the cockpit of a spaceship?
Put a bucket of manure in the
passenger compartment.

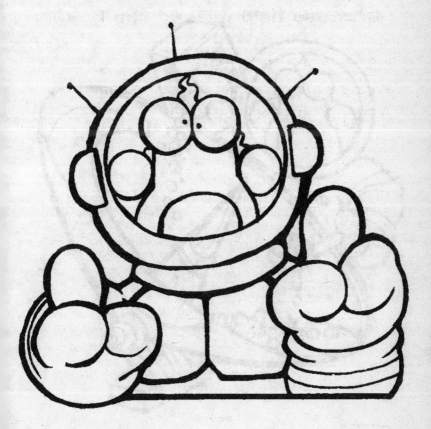

When does a spaceman have his midday meal?
At launch time.

284

What's furry, silly, and found on Mars? A lost Zoggian.

Where do you leave a spaceship on the moon?
At a parking meteor.

What's large, purple and eats spaceships?
A large, purple spaceship eater.

285

**What's large,
purple and eats
space buggies?
A large, purple
spaceship eater on
a diet.**

What's large, purple and
eats cabbage?
A vegetarian large purple
spaceship eater.

**How do you know
if an elephant is
piloting your
spaceship?
By the large E on
his helmet.**

286

What's ten feet tall, furry and related to Zig and Zag?
A Zoggian on stilts.

FIRST ASTRONAUT: Good journey?
SECOND ASTRONAUT: Yes. Everything went well except for one thing.
FIRST ASTRONAUT: What was that?
SECOND ASTRONAUT: Well, you know my waterproof, shockproof, rustproof watch?
FIRST ASTRONAUT: Yes?
SECOND ASTRONAUT: Well, it caught fire.

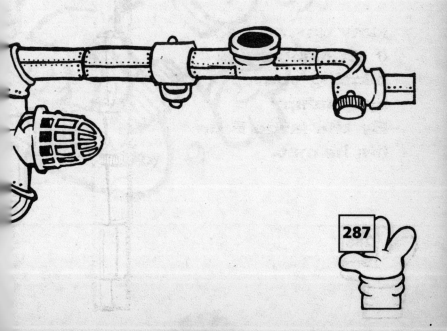

What's yellow and travels at 1000 miles an hour?

288

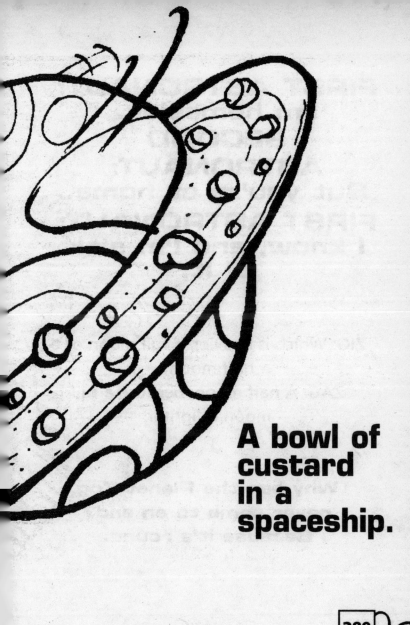

**A bowl of
custard
in a
spaceship.**

FIRST ASTRONAUT:
I'm homesick.
SECOND
ASTRONAUT:
But you're at home.
FIRST ASTRONAUT:
I know, and I'm sick
of it.

ZIG: Which is heavier, a full moon or a
half moon?
ZAG: A half moon, because a full
moon is lighter.

Why can the Planet Zog
never come to an end?
Because it's round.

What's a Zoggian worm?
A Zoggian centipede with
no legs.

ZIG: Why was there a puddle on the spaceship floor?

ZAG: That was where the centi-peed.

Where are Martian kings and queens crowned?
On the head, of course!

What do eggs in outer space hate to see?
Unidentified Frying Omelettes.

Why is a spaceship silver and rocket-shaped?
Because if it were yellow and curved it would be a banana.

Why did the invisible spaceman look in the mirror?
To see if he still wasn't there.

What's purple, green and weightless?
Zag in outer space.

What's fawn, furry and travels around in a
moon buggy?
Zig on holiday.

ZIG: Can I have a ticket to Zog for my friend Zag?
TICKET SELLER: I'm sorry sir, we don't do swaps.

What's blue and white and sits in the space station kitchen?
A fridge wearing jeans.

What happens to a Zoggian when it rains?
He gets wet.

Why does a spaceman wear a helmet?
Because he'd look silly in a flowery hat.

Knock, knock.
Who's there?
Jupiter.

298

Jupiter who?
Jupiter spider in
my shoes?

Who won the space monster beauty contest?
Nobody!

What's the difference between a space monster and spaghetti?
A space monster won't slip off your fork.

LITTLE SPACE MONSTER:
Mum! When will supper be ready?
MUM SPACE MONSTER: You'll just have to be patient, Zork, I've only got three pairs of hands!

What did the space
helmet say to the
scarf?
You hang around while
I go on ahead.

Zig and Zag Back Home

ZOGALISTIC

ZANIES!

What's found in the salad drawer and plays pop music?
A transistor lettuce.

What's yellow and goes putt, putt, putt?
An outboard lemon.

What's purple and green and crying in the kitchen?
Zag chopping onions.

What's purple and green and fawn and furry
and snoozing?
Zig and Zag watching a boring TV programme.

305

CEILING SUCKER STILT WALKIN'

306

What has a head, four legs but only one
foot, and is found in a house?
A bed.

Which famous painter had two bathrooms in his house?
Two-loos Lautrec.

What kind of animal did baby Jim look
like in the bath?
A little bear.

What do you call a woman with a
gas fire on her head?
Anita.

What do you call a woman with
two lavatories on her head?
Lulu.

What do you call a woman with
tiles on her head?
Ruth.

What do you call a woman with a
Christmas tree on her head?
Carol.

When is a chair like a fabric?
When it's sat in.

What did the floor say to the desk?
'Watch out, I can see your drawers!'

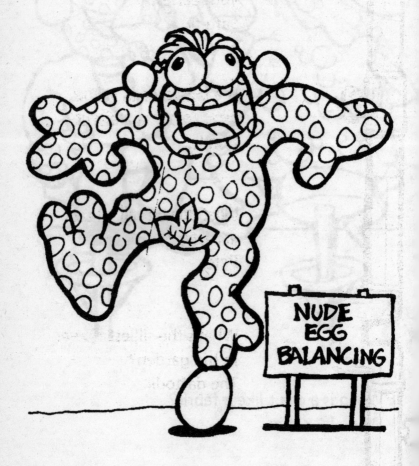

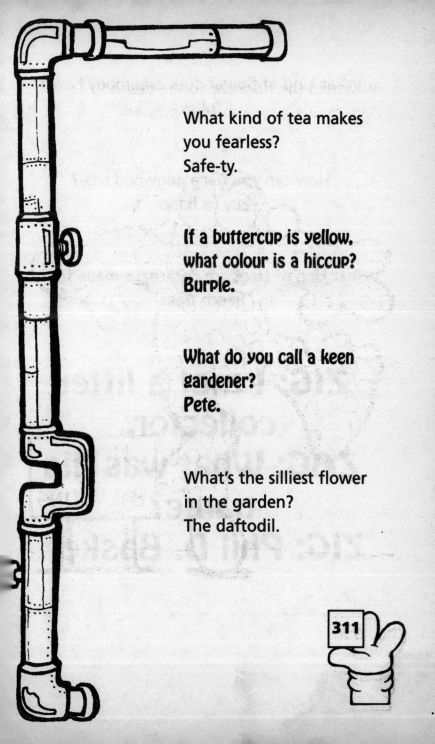

What kind of tea makes
you fearless?
Safe-ty.

If a buttercup is yellow,
what colour is a hiccup?
Burple.

What do you call a keen
gardener?
Pete.

What's the silliest flower
in the garden?
The daftodil.

What kind of flower does everybody have?
Tulips.

How can you tell a dogwood tree?
By its bark.

What kind of trees are deckchairs made from?
Beech trees.

ZIG: I met a litter collector.
ZAG: What was his name?
ZIG: Phil D. Basket.

Why did Zig put his bed in the fireplace?
Because he wanted to sleep like a log.

BILL: Are you a light sleeper?
BEN: No, I sleep in the dark.

313

ZIG: Time to get up! It's 7.30!
ZAG: Who's winning?

314

Why did the idiot sleep under his car?
So he would wake up oily in the morning.

What do cornflakes wear on their feet?
K'logs.

ZAG: How does a coffee pot feel when
it's full?
ZIG: I don't know.
ZAG: Perky!

How do you use an Egyptian doorbell?
Toot-and-come-in.

CUSTOMER: Have you any of that striped wallpaper?
SALESMAN: Yes, sir.
CUSTOMER: Can I put it on myself?
SALESMAN: Yes, but it would look better on the wall.

What do French children have for breakfast?
Huit heures bix.

How can you tell the time with candles?
By the candles' tick.

MRS FUSSY: I must go home now. Don't trouble to see me to the door.
MRS NASTY: It's no trouble – it'll be a pleasure.

What's purple and green, purple and green, purple and green!
Zag falling down the stairs.

What's fawn, furry and laughing?
Zig, because he pushed him.

Hickory dickory dock.
An elephant ran up the clock.
The clock is now being repaired.

**Knock, knock.
Who's there?
Plato.
Plato who?
Plato fish and chips.**

**Knock, knock.
Who's there?
Canoe.
Canoe who?
Canoe come out and play?**

**Knock, knock.
Who's there?
Dwayne.
Dwayne who?
Dwayne the bath, I'm
dwowning.**

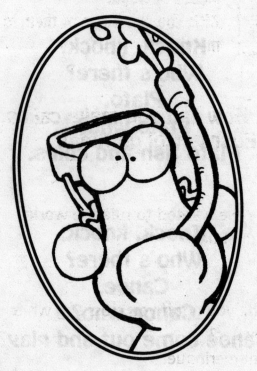

'Eureka!' cried the mad scientist.
'You don't smell too good yourself,'
replied Zig.

**ZAG: Can you light a fire with two
pieces of wood?
ZIG: You can if one of them is a
match.**

ZAG: How can you make cakes light?
ZIG: Pour petrol on them.

Which cake wanted to rule the world?
Attila the Bun.

What do you get if you cross egg white with
gunpowder?
A boom-meringue.

What's grey and comes at you from all sides?
Quadrophonic porridge.

What's orange and shoots?
A double-barrelled carrot.

What's yellow and buzzes?
An electric banana.

What's green and signs cheques?
A ballpoint cucumber.

Who invented the first fireplace?
Alfred the Grate.

What do butterflies sleep on?
Caterpillows.

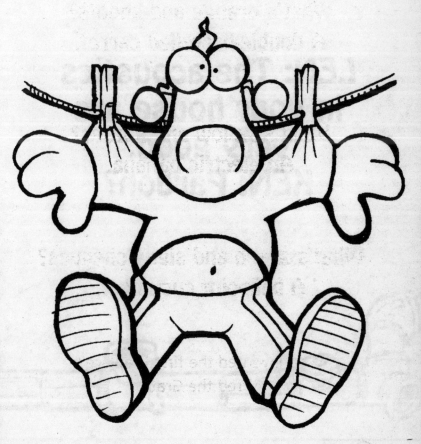

ZIG: What would you do if you heard a mouse squeak in the night?
ZAG: I don't know, but I wouldn't get up to oil it.

LEN: The acoustics in your house are very good.
KEN: Pardon?

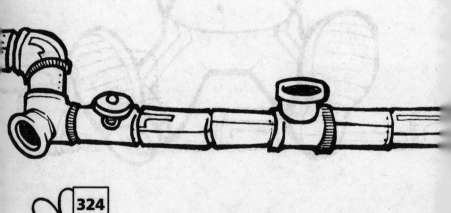

324

ZAG: Did you hear about the new deodorant called 'Vanish'?
ZIG: Is it any good?
ZAG: It certainly is. You spray it on then disappear – and no one knows where the smell's coming from!

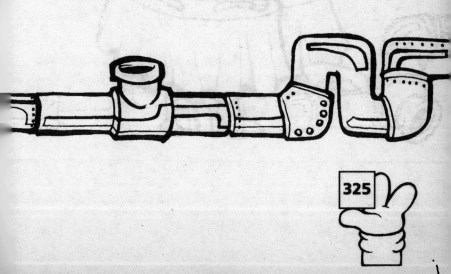

325

How do you make antifreeze?
Hide her thermal underwear.

How do you
make an
apple puff?
Chase it round
the garden.

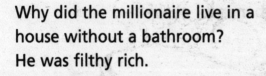

Why did the millionaire live in a
house without a bathroom?
He was filthy rich.

ZIG: How's your nose?
ZAG: Shut up!
ZIG: So's mine. Must be
the weather

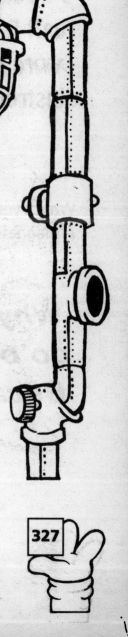

327

Did you hear what happened when daft Dave painted his house? He wore three jackets because the instructions on the tin said 'Put on three coats.'

What's yellow and always points north?
A magnetic banana.

Why did the banana go out with a prune? Because he couldn't find a date.

ANGRY NEIGHBOUR: What are you doing up my apple tree?
NAUGHTY BOY: One of your apples fell down and I was trying to put it back.

329

Why did the biscuit cry?
Because his mother had been a wafer so long.

Why did the window pane blush?
Because it saw the weatherstrip.

Why did Zig buy some
red braces?
Because he was a messy
spaghetti eater.

GREAT-AUNT HARRIET: You're very
quiet, Belinda.
BELINDA: Yes. Mum
gave me 50p not to
say anything about
your glass eye.

**What do you get if you
mow over a budgie?
Shredded tweet.**

331

ZIG: What do you mean by telling everyone I'm a nutcase?
ZAG: I didn't know it was meant to be a secret.

ZAG: Are you superstitious?
ZIG: No.
ZAG: Then lend me £13.

What's yellow, brown and hairy?
Cheese on toast dropped on the carpet.

What were Tarzan's last words?
Who greased that vine?

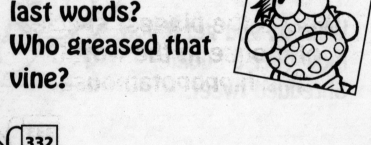

What's the biggest species of mouse in the world?'
The hippopotamouse.

333

What's green and slimy and goes hith?
A snake with a lisp.

334

What's yellow and black with red spots?
A leopard with measles.

What's black and white and noisy?
A zebra with a set of drums.

What's white, furry, and smells of peppermint?
A polo bear.

What's blue and flies through the trees? Tarzan in a boiler suit.

What animal do you eat for pudding? A moose.

What do you call a gorilla with a tommy-gun? Sir.

What's grey and white
and red all over?
An embarrassed
elephant.

341

What do you give an elephant who is stressed out? Trunquillizers.

What did the river say to the elephant when he sat in it?
'Well, I'll be damned.'

Can an elephant jump higher than
a lamp-post?
Yes. Lamp-posts can't jump.

'Doctor, doctor, I keep thinking I'm invisible.'
'Who said that?'

'Doctor, doctor, I feel like a five-pound note.'
'Go shopping, the change will do you good.'

'Doctor, doctor, I feel like a pack of cards.'
'Sit down and I'll deal with you later.'

345

Doctor, doctor, I keep seeing striped camels.'
'Have you ever seen a psychiatrist?'
'No, I only see striped camels.'

'Doctor, doctor, I feel like a cricket ball.'
'How's that?'
'Don't you start.'

'Doctor, doctor, I keep thinking I'm a goat.'
'How long have you had this feeling?'
'Since I was a kid.'

'Doctor, doctor, I keep thinking I'm a dustbin.'
'Don't talk rubbish.'

347

'Doctor, doctor, what can I do, my little boy has swallowed my pen?'
'Use a pencil till I get there.'

'Doctor, doctor, everyone thinks I'm a liar.'
'I don't believe you.'

PATIENT: 'Doctor, doctor, everyone keeps being rude to me.'
DOCTOR: 'Get out of here you silly fool.'

MAN: 'Ouch! A crab just bit my toe.'
Doctor: 'Which one?'
MAN: 'I don't know, all crabs look alike to me.'

'Doctor, doctor, will you
help me out?'
'Certainly, which way did
you come in?'

'Doctor, doctor, I think
I'm a clock.'
'Well, don't get wound
up about it.'

'Doctor, Doctor, I have a terrible
problem. I keep stealing things.'
'Have you been taking anything
for it?'

349

What kind of fish is most useful on ice?
A skate.

What do a dentist and a farmer have in common?
They both deal in acres (achers).

What kind of fish do you find in a bird-cage?
A perch.

How can you tell that fish are musical? Everyone knows about the piano tuna.

What menaces the deep and plays the banjo?
Jaws Formby.

Why are fishmongers so mean?
Because their job makes them shellfish.

351

What's the best way to catch a fish?
Get someone to throw one to you.

Where would a man post a letter in his
sleep?
In a pillow-box.

Where do elves go to get fit?
Elf farms.

How does a fireplace feel when you fill it with coal?
Grate-full.

How many weeks belong to a year? Forty-six. The other six are only Lent.

Shall I tell you the joke about the bed?
No, it hasn't been made yet.

Keep smiling. It makes everybody wonder what you're up to.

353

What is an octopus?
An eight-sided cat.

Did you hear about the man who stole some rhubarb?
He was put into custardy.

'I've lost my dog.'
'Why don't you put an advertisement in the paper?'
'Don't be silly – he can't read.'

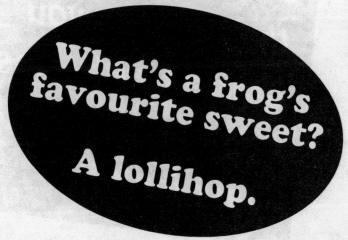

What's a frog's favourite sweet?

A lollihop.

Think of a number between one and fifty. Double it, subtract sixty-one, add one, subtract the number you started with, close your eyes . . . Dark isn't it!

356

BULLDOG FOR SALE.
Will eat anything – very fond of children.

What do cats strive for?
Purrfection.

What do you call a cat that sucks acid drops?
A sour puss.

What's worse than raining cats and dogs? Hailing taxis.

When is a brown dog not a brown dog?
When it's a greyhound.

When is it bad luck to have a black cat follow you?
When you are a mouse.

358

What book was written by a cat?
The Thoughts of Meou Tse Tung.

FIRST CLEVER DICK: 'Every day my dog and I go for a tramp in the woods.'
SECOND CLEVER DICK: 'Does the dog enjoy it?'
FIRST CLEVER DICK: 'Yes, but the tramp's getting a bit fed up.'

What are blue-blooded, short-legged, and live in a palace?
The Queen's corgi dogs.

What did the cowboy say to his dog when it fell off the cliff?
Dawg gone.

359

Do you know the joke about the cornflakes and the shredded wheat who had a fight? I can only tell you a little, as it's a serial.

When should a mouse carry an umbrella?
When it's raining cats and dogs.

What's the fastest thing in the world?
Milk – because it's past your eyes before
you see it.

**What's the difference between a night watchman and a butcher?
One stays awake and the other weighs a steak.**

Why are cooks cruel?
They beat eggs, whip cream and batter fish.

What did the traffic warden have in his sandwiches?
Traffic jam.

What do jelly-babies wear on their feet? Gum-boots.

What happened to the man who couldn't tell putty from porridge?
His windows fell out.

362

ZIG: A dog bit my ankle yesterday.
ZAG: Did you put anything on it?
ZIG: No, he seemed to like it just as it was.

What's huge, icy and tastes delicious?
A glacier mint.

When is a red-headed idiot like a biscuit?
When he's a ginger nut.

What's a lawyer's favourite pudding?
Sue-it.

What tree has the best food?
A pantry.

What happens to bikes when they get old? They get recycled.

Who was the first person to wear a shell suit? Humpty Dumpty.

364

Why did the baker stop making doughnuts? Because he got tired of the hole business.

What's white and fluffy and beats its chest in a cake shop?
A meringue-utang.

How do you know a sausage doesn't like being fried?
Because it spits.

What did the hamburger say to the tomato? That's enough of your sauce.

Should you stir your tea with your left hand or right?
Neither. You should stir it with a spoon.

What goes 100 m.p.h. on the railway lines and is yellow and white?
A train driver's egg sandwich.

How can you stop food going bad? Eat it.

What swings about a cake-shop yodelling?
Tarzipan.

What do you call a lazy Stegosaurus?
A Stegosnaurus.

What's purple and flies in outer space?
Planet of the grapes.

What lives in pods and is a Kung Fu expert?
Bruce Pea.

Why is it dangerous to play cards in the jungle?
Because there are so many cheetahs.

What do you get if you cross a centipede
with a parrot?
A walkie-talkie.

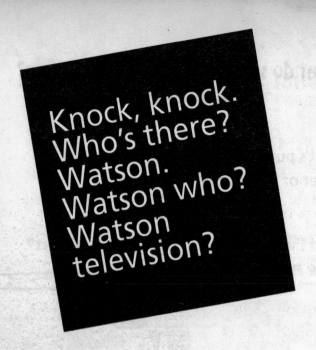

Knock, knock.
Who's there?
Watson.
Watson who?
Watson television?

What spins and does not stop?
The world.

What does the invisible man call his mum and dad? Transparents.

368

What is big and red and eats rocks?
A big red rock eater.

What's black and white and black and white and black and white?
A puffin rolling downhill.

And what's black and white and laughing?
The second puffin who pushed the first one down the hill.

Knock, knock.
Who's there?
Madam.
Madam who?
Ma damn fist's stuck in the door.

369

**What's white and dashes through
the desert with a bed-pan?
Florence of Arabia.**

What do you feed under-nourished dwarfs?
Elf-raising flour.

What do you call a
frog spy?
A croak and dagger
agent.

What goes croak!
croak! when it's misty?
A frog-horn.

What do you get if
you cross a frog and
a can of cola?
Croak-a-cola.

What runs but never moves?
A fence.

What is a good name for the wife of an engineer?
Bridget.

What's higher than an admiral?
His hat.

What do you call a Scottish cloakroom-
attendant?
Angus McCoatup.

Knock, knock.
Who's there?
Tish.
Tish who?
'Bless you!'

Knock, knock.
Who's there?
Dismay.
Dismay who?
Dismay be a joke but it doesn't make me laugh.

What's yellow and goes 'slam, slam, slam, slam'?
A four-door banana.

What do you do if you find a blue banana?
Try to cheer it up.

Why don't you tell secrets in vegetable gardens?
Because corn has ears and beans talk.

Knock, knock.
Who's there?
Cook.
Cook who?
That's the first one I've heard this year.

How do you calculate the colour
of plums?
Use a green gauge.

375

Knock, knock.
Who's there?
Granny.
Knock, knock.
Who's there?
Granny.
Knock, knock.
Who's there?
Granny.
Knock, knock.
Who's there?
Aunt.
Aunt who?
Aunt you glad I got rid of all those grannies?

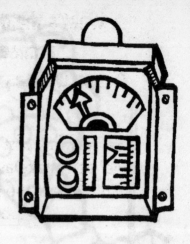

Why did the farmer call his rooster Robinson?
Because he crew so.

What sort of musical instrument did Ancient
Britons play?
The Anglo Saxophone.

376

What's the definition of an archaeologist?
A man whose career is in ruins.

Take away my first letter, take away my second letter, take away all my letters and I still remain the same. What am I?
A postman.

What kind of ears does a train have?
Engineers.

What is a Fjord?
A Norwegian motor car.

UNCLE: Who was that at the door?
JANE: The Invisible Man.
UNCLE: Tell him I can't see him.

377

If I dug a hole in the middle of the road, what would come up?
A policeman.

What do policemen have in their sandwiches?
Truncheon meat.

Why are policemen strong?
Because they can hold up traffic.

Why did the policeman cry?
Because he couldn't take his panda to bed.

What's red, runs on wheels, and eats grass?
A bus.
PS I lied about the grass.

Where do tadpoles go when they lose their tails?
To a retail shop.

How can you tell which end of a worm is his head?
Tickle his middle and see which end smiles.

How many letters are there in a space alphabet?
Only 24 – ET went home.

What letters are bad for your teeth?
D.K. (decay).

Robinson Publishing,
PO Box 11, Falmouth, Cornwall TR10 9EN
Tel: +44(0) 1326 317200 Fax: +44(0) 1326 317444
Email: books@Barni.avel.co.uk

UK/B.F.P.O. customers please allow £1.00 for p&p for the
first book, plus 50p for the second, plus 30p for each
additional book up to a maximum charge of £3.
Overseas customers (inc. Ireland), please allow £2.00 for
the first book plus £1.00 for the second, plus 50p for each
additional book.

Please send me:

☐ **Horse Stories**   £4.99   ☐ **Fantasy Stories**   £4.99
☐ **Dance Stories**   £4.99   ☐ **Space Stories**   £4.99
☐ **The Joke Museum** £3.99

NAME (Block Letters)...

ADDRESS...

....

....POSTCODE...............................

I enclose a cheque/PO
(payable to Robinson Publishing Ltd) for..............................

I wish to pay by Switch/Credit card

Number...

Card Expiry Date..